Tom Osborne

Through thirty-plus years of coaching and working with the Teammates Mentoring Program, I've come to believe that we're living in a very difficult age for children. Many families are not as stable as they once were. Movies and the internet carry images which would have been unthinkable not long ago and the drug culture has invaded lives at early ages. Many children are not imbued with foundational principles which enable them to navigate this difficult terrain. This short book is an effort to provide an avenue for caregivers to discuss ideas which will be helpful to children as they try to steer the difficult years of childhood on their journey to successful adulthood.

Each child is unique and has special talents. It is important to have them recognize and build on their strengths. When I was coaching, I often was able to encourage a player in such a way that he grew into the athlete he had no idea he could become, simply by making him aware of talents he could not see himself. Everyone needs someone who loves them unconditionally and is a person they can turn to for encouragement and advice. Unfortunately, many of our young people do not have that person.

Life is not easy. One thing that athletics teaches is that there will be adversity along the way, and adversity is a great teacher. The only constructive way to deal with adversity is not to blame others for misfortune, or to give up, but rather to see it as an opportunity to learn and improve. This requires hard work and perseverance. Many of our best players were not the most talented, but they had unusual tenacity and willpower and they worked very hard to overcome their deficiencies.

Many young people are not grounded in the understanding that God loves them, understands them and wants the best for them. Hardship and obstacles sometimes are ways of getting our attention and causing us to grow in our faith. If we live according to His principles, we will become better able to serve others and live lives which are full of meaning and purpose. Wealth, trophies and praise from others are often not what they seem to be. Knowing you served God in the best way that you could is the most fulfilling way to live.

Tom Osborne

All rights reserved. No part of this book
may be reproduced or utilized in
any form or by any means electronic or mechanical
including photocopying, recording, or by
any information storage and retrieval system
without permission in writing from the
publisher, Kraken Books Limited.

© 2020 Kraken Books
Text © Tom Osborne
with Jefferson Knapp
Illustrations © Sergio Drumond
Published and produced by
Kraken Books Ltd.
1019 Skyview Drive
El Dorado, KS 67042

For more information on this book,
please check out
www.krakenbooks.com

ISBN 978-0-9969742-5-7

Printed in the
United States of America
10 9 8 7 6 5 4 3 2 1

"To my wife Nancy"

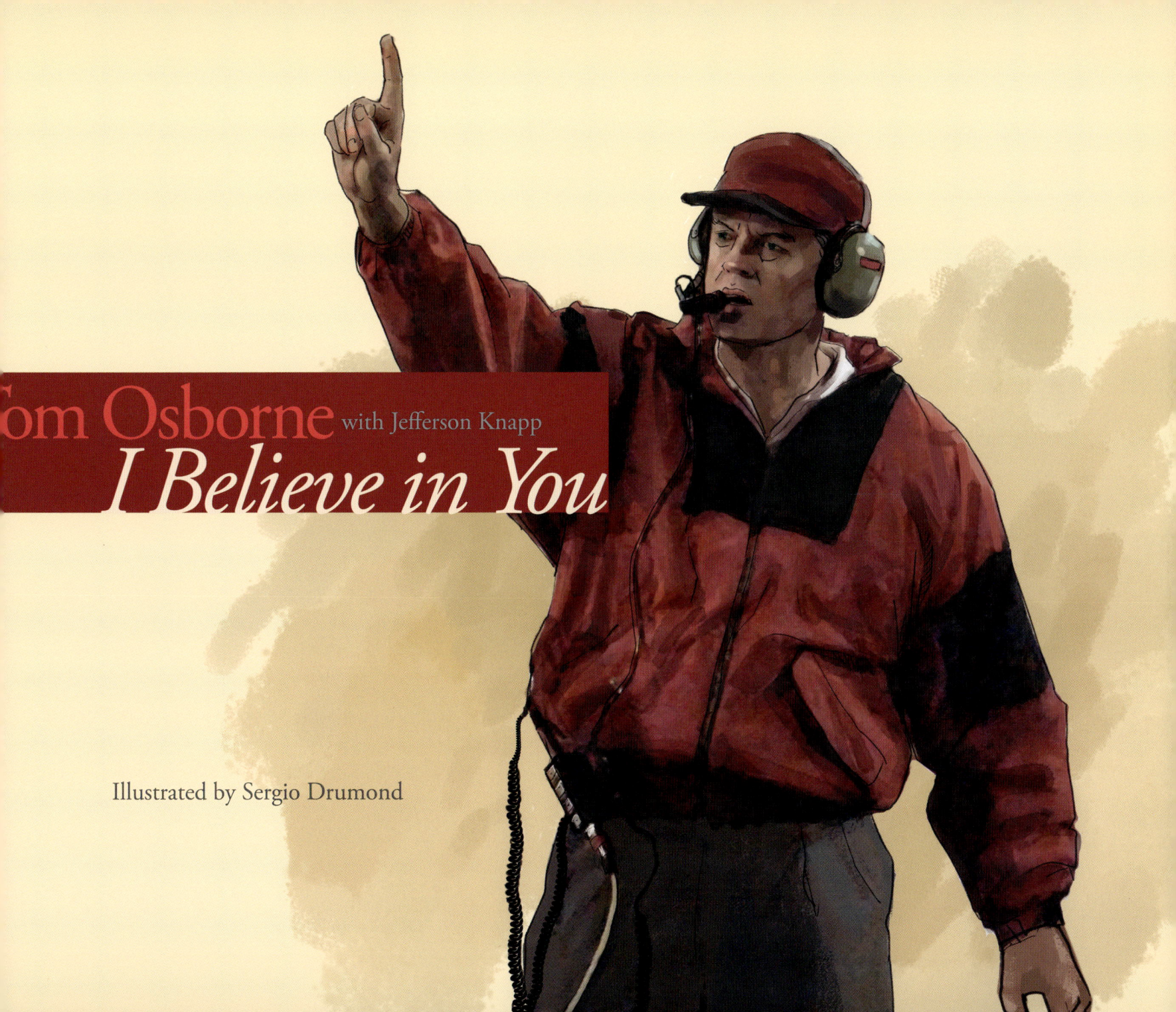

Tom Osborne with Jefferson Knapp
I Believe in You

Illustrated by Sergio Drumond

We are going through tough times right now,
But there's one thing I know is true.

You were created to make a difference in this world,

And I believe in you.

It wasn't easy being a kid,

I know things have changed a lot. But obstacles and roadblocks will always be there,

Whether you like it or not.

There are
no short cuts in life,
Especially when chasing your dreams.

Don't be misled by another's accomplishments,

Success isn't always
as it seems.

When you finally have that goal in your heart,
Don't be afraid to fail.
Not doing it easy but the hard way,
That is the story you'll tell.

So, what do you do when times get tough,

And the wall seems impossible to climb?

Unite yourself to like-minded friends,

And give them your commitment and time.

If you do the right thing every day,

And keep the fundamentals sound.

Then winning will take care of itself,

Up till the last go around.

No matter what you do give it your all,
Even when the odds have you beat.

And be humble when you overcome, And gracious in victory and defeat.

Don't settle for mediocrity,
Make integrity who you are.
There is no choice but to go for the win,
Forget the moon and aim for the stars.

When things don't work, work harder.

This will produce all that is good.

With mental toughness and a positive attitude,

You'll do things you never thought you could.

When you focus and give maximum effort,

You have already won.

Stay out of trouble and remember to laugh,

The journey should always be fun.

The process is more enjoyable than the end result,

So, keep the drill work right.

Great work ethic is invaluable,

Always keep consistency in sight.

You never know how much time is left,

Walk away while you can still can.

Moments that have brought much joy in life, Were worth the race that I ran.

So, don't you worry about the next bad thing,

Trials will come and leave.

Focus your life on faith and family,

And don't be afraid to believe.

Because no matter what we face in life,
Here is some wonderful news—

The Almighty Savior that I believe in, Also believes in you, too!

Dear Reader,

Life is often difficult. Please remember that you are not alone. There is always someone willing to help, a family member, a teacher, a coach, a friend who will be there for you.

Don't be afraid to reach out and let important people in your life know what you are feeling and what you want to accomplish. They will help you.

God bless you as you grow into the person you can be.

Tom Osborne

10-6-2022

Caden,

You are the bright light in the room! Your infectious personality makes everyone happier! It's God's gift, use it.

You are a good person, handsome, smart and witty. I know you will always be kind and caring and will be there to help everyone, as God leads you.

Love You
Papa Pat